Nita Mehta's
Everyday Khaana

Vegetarian

100% TRIED & TESTED RECIPES

Nita Mehta

B.Sc. (Home Science), M.Sc. (Food and Nutrition) Gold Medalist

Tanya Mehta

SNAB
Excellence in Books

Nita Mehta's
Everyday Khaana

4th Print 2009

ISBN 978-81-7869-085-8

Food Styling and Photography: **SNAB**

Layout and laser typesetting :

National Information Technology Academy
N.I.T.A. 3A/3, Asaf Ali Road, New Delhi-110002
☎ 23252948

Contributing Writers :
Anurag Mehta
Subhash Mehta

Editorial & Proofreading :
Rakesh
Ramesh

Published by :

SNAB
Excellence in Books
Publishers Pvt. Ltd.
3A/3 Asaf Ali Road,
New Delhi - 110002
Tel: 23252948, 23250091
Telefax: 91-11-23250091

Editorial and Marketing office:
E-159, Greater Kailash-II, N.Delhi-48
Fax: 91-11-29225218, 29229558
Tel: 91-11-29214011, 29218574
E-Mail: nitamehta@email.com
nitamehta@nitamehta.com
Website: http://www.nitamehta.com
Website: http://www.snabindia.com

Distributed by :
THE VARIETY BOOK DEPOT
A.V.G. Bhavan, M 3 Con Circus,
New Delhi - 110 001
Tel : 23417175, 23412567; Fax : 23415335
Email: varietybookdepot@rediffmail.com

Printed by :
DEVTECH PUBLISHERS & PRINTERS PVT LTD

Rs. 89/-

Introduction

$\mathcal{W}$ ho wants to eat a heavy, spicy meal everyday? Such meals can be taken just once in a while. Everyday food besides being delicious should be light, healthy and quick to prepare. Many women think that unless you put in hours in the kitchen, the food will not be really appreciated. This book has quick, simple, yet delicious recipes which will be well rewarded.

The recipes have been very thoughtfully divided into breakfast, lunch and dinner. The book also offers a few simple low cal desserts which will satisfy that sweet craving. We truly believe that home cooked meals are the best. Here is an attempt to make you and your family also believe the same.

Nita Mehta

ABOUT THE RECIPES

WHAT'S IN A CUP?

INDIAN CUP
1 teacup = 200 ml liquid
AMERICAN CUP
1 cup = 240 ml liquid (8 oz.)
The recipes in this book were tested with the Indian teacup which holds 200 ml liquid.

CONTENTS

LUNCH - CURRIES & DRY 28

Chhole Bhature   29
Matar Paneer   32
Rajmah   34
Sambar   36
Gobhi Aloo   40

Gajar Matar   42
Kale Chane Rasse Waale   44
Saffed Chhole-Rasse Waale   46
Simla Mirch Aloo   50
Matar Aloo   52

DINNER CURRIES & DRY 54

Kati Arbi   55
Channe ki Dal with Ghiya   56
Paneer Makhani   60
Koftas in Green Gravy   62
Mixed Dal   64
Kati Bhindi   65

Baingan ka Bharta   66
Bharwaan Karele   70
Dal Makhani   72
Special Mixed Subzi   74
Paalak Paneer   76
Kadhai Babycorns   80

8

RICE, ROTI AND RAITAS 83

SWEET DISHES 98

BREAKFAST

Weekend Aloo-Poori Nashta

The Sunday Indian breakfast needs no introduction!

Picture on page 20   *Serves 4*

ALOO KI SUBZI

6 potatoes - boiled, peeled and each cut into 6 pieces, mash the pieces roughly

3½ tbsp ghee or oil

3 pinches of hing (asafoetida)

¾ tsp jeera (cumin seeds), 1 tsp saunf (fennel)

¼ tsp methi dana (fenugreek seeds)

½ tsp haldi powder, 1 tsp dhania powder

1½ tsp salt, ¾ tsp red chilli powder

1 tbsp aam ke achar ka masala

1 tsp very finely chopped or grated ginger

1 green chilli - finely chopped

2 tbsp chopped coriander (hara dhania)

1. For the subzi, heat ghee in a kadhai. Collect together hing, jeera, saunf and methi dana. Reduce heat. Add all spices together.
2. When methi dana turns brown, add haldi, dhania powder, salt and red chilli powder. Bhuno for 5-10 seconds on low heat.
3. Add achar ka masala and ginger. Stir for 1 minute.
4. Add the potatoes, chopped green chilli and coriander. Stir fry on medium heat for 3-4 minutes.
5. Add 3 cups of water. Bring to a boil. Reduce heat and cook covered for another 10 minutes. Remove from fire. Serve hot with poori, given on next page.

Poori

Serves 4   *Picture on page 20*

2 cups atta (whole wheat flour), 1 tsp salt
2 tsp ghee, oil for frying

1. Sift flour and salt together. Add melted ghee and mix well.
2. Knead to a firm dough with water. Cover and keep aside for 15-20 minutes.
3. Divide dough into small balls and roll out the balls into small rounds using little oil.
4. Heat oil for frying in a kadhai. Drop rolled poori gently into it, press the sides of the poori with a perforated frying spoon and turn. Fry till golden brown. Drain on paper napkins.
5. Fry the second puri in the same way. Serve with aloo ki subzi.

Bread Pakora

Sandwiched slices of bread coated with besan. If you like you can simply dip the bread slices in the besan batter and make besan waale toasts - a favourite of my son when he was a small child. He now heads this publishing house. Those crisp besan coated toasts remind me of those wonderful years!

Picture on page 1   *Serves 2*

6 slices of bread

BATTER

1 cup besan (gramflour), ¾ - 1 cup water
1 tsp garam masala, ½ tsp red chilli powder
½ tsp haldi, 1 tsp salt

FILLING

2 potatoes (aloos) - boiled, peeled and grated
¼ tsp red chilli powder, ¼ tsp amchoor
¼ tsp bhuna jeera powder (roasted cumin powder)
½ tsp dhania powder, ½ tsp salt, 2 tbsp chopped onion
1 green chilli - deseeded & chopped

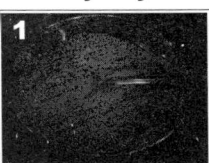

1. Mix all the ingredients of batter in a flat dish. Mix well with a baloon whisk or a karchi to break all the lumps.
2. Mix all ingredients of filling in a bowl. Mix well.
3. Divide the filling into 6 portions.
4. Cut each bread slice into two triangles. Spread 1 portion of filling on each bread. Press the filling with fingers.

5. Put the other triangle piece of bread on it. Press well to stick together.
6. Heat 5-6 tbsp oil in a non stick pan or add ½ cup oil in a kadhai.
7. Dip the sandwiched bread in the batter, immediately put it in the oil.

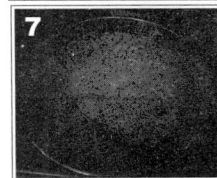

8. Shallow fry the bread on both sides until light brown. Drain on paper napkin.
9. Serve hot with tomato sauce or poodina chutney.

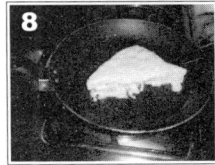

Upma

The South Indian breakfast. Enjoy it with a good cup of coffee.

Picture on page 1   *Serves 6*

1½ cups suji (semolina), try using the moti suji or rawa
1 tsp sarson (mustard seeds)
2-3 dried red chillies (sookhi lal mirch)
1½ tbsp channe ki dal (split gram)
1 tbsp urad dhuli dal (split black beans)
2 onions - chopped finely
3½ cups water
½ cup shelled, boiled or frozen peas (matar)
juice of 1 large lemon
1½ tsp salt
10-12 curry leaves - optional
5 tbsp oil

1. Dry roast suji in a kadahi on low flame, stirring continuously, for about 5 minutes. Do not let it change colour and turn brownish. Let it be whitish. Remove from fire and keep aside.
2. In a clean heavy bottomed kadhai, heat oil. Reduce heat. Add sarson.
3. Remove from fire. Add the dry red chilli and dal. Stir till dal turns light brown.
4. Return to fire. Add onions. Fry till onions turn brown.
5. Add water. Add peas, salt and lemon juice. Boil water.
6. Cover and cook on low flame for 5-7 minutes till the dal is cooked and is no longer crunchy.
7. Keeping the flame low, add suji gradually with one hand, stirring with the other hand continuously.
8. After all the suji has been added, stir fry the upma for 2-3 minutes.
9. Add 2 more tsp oil and fry for another minute.
10. To serve, transfer some hot upma in a steel katori. Press lightly. Place the serving plate on the katori and holding the katori in one hand and pressing the plate with the other hand, invert the katori on to the plate to get a heap of upma for an individual serving.

Matar Dalia

Sweet dalia with milk sounds so boring! An alternate way of enjoying the most healthy food.

Picture on facing page   *Serves 3-4*

½ cup dalia (broken wheat) - soaked in water for at least
½ hour or more, ½ cup shelled peas (matar)
1 green chilli - deseeded & chopped
1 small potato - peeled & cut into very small pieces
2 tbsp oil ½ tsp jeera (cumin seeds)
4-5 saboot kali mirch (peppercorns) - crushed
½" piece ginger - finely chopped (1 tsp), 1 tej patta (bay leaf)
1 chhoti illaichi (green cardamom) - crushed
¼ tsp haldi (turmeric powder), 1 tsp salt
¼ tsp red chilli powder, 1 tbsp lemon juice
2 tbsp chopped coriander, ¼ tsp garam masala

1.   Wash and soak dalia in enough water for about an hour or more.

Contd...

2. Cut potato into very tiny cubes.
3. Heat 2 tbsp oil in a non stick kadhai or a pan. Add ½ tsp jeera. Let it turn golden.

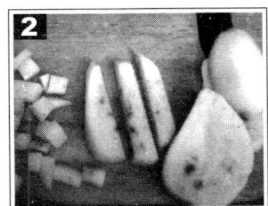

4. Add crushed saboot kali mirch, ginger, tej patta and illaichi together. Reduce flame.
5. Add potatoes and stir fry for 2 minutes.
6. Add haldi, salt and red chilli powder. Mix.
7. Add peas and green chilli. Bhuno the vegetables for 1 minute on low flame.

8. Drain the dalia through a fine strainer and add to the vegetables. Stir fry for 2 minutes.
9. Cover tightly and cook further for 5 minutes, stirring occasionally. Cook till potatoes and peas turn soft.
10. Remove from fire. Mix in the lemon juice, coriander and garam masala. Serve hot.

Note: Cook dalia in a non stick utensil, otherwise it sticks to the bottom of the utensil while cooking.

◁ *Puri : Recipe on page 11*
◁ *Weekend Aloo-Poori Nashta : Recipe on page 12*

Masala Pooda

A protein rich breakfast of gramflour pancakes (besan poodas). The hari chutney can be made a couple of days in advance and refrigerated.

Picture on page 38   *Makes 2*

BATTER

1 cup besan (gram flour)
1 cup water (approx.)
1 tsp kasoori methi (dry fenugreek leaves)
½ tsp red chilli powder
¾ tsp salt
1 small onion - very finely chopped
1 small tomato - very finely chopped
1 green chilli - deseeded & very finely chopped
1 tbsp chopped coriander, salt, pepper to taste

1. Mix all ingredients of the batter together in a bowl. Beat well to make a batter of pouring consistency.
2. Heat a non stick pan (not too hot). Smear 1 tsp oil in the centre.
3. Remove from fire and spread 1½ karchhis of batter (½ of the batter). Spread by tilting the pan.
4. Return to fire. After 1 minute, when the edges get slightly cooked, add 1 tsp of oil on the sides.
5. When the top is cooked, add a few drops of oil on the top of the pooda.
6. Turn over when the underside is done. Cook the other side.
7. Fold into half. Serve immediately with tomato ketchup or mint chutney.

Mini Rawa Oothapam

These thick South Indian pancakes can be prepared without having to wait for the batter to ferment. The sour curd and soda bi carb take care of the lightness without fermentation.

Picture on page 2   *Makes 5-6*

BATTER

1½ cups rava or moti suji (coarse semolina)
1½ cups sour curd (khatti dahi), ¾ cup water
¼ tsp mitha soda (soda-bi-carb), 1 tsp salt
¼ tsp hing (asafoetida powder)

TOPPING

1-2 green chillies - chopped
a few curry leaves - chopped
2 onions - chopped
2 tomatoes - chopped
1 carrot - grated
salt to taste

1. Mix all ingredients of the batter together.
2. Add enough water to the batter to get a thick pouring consistency. Beat well.
3. Keep the batter aside for ½ hour.
4. At serving time, add mitha soda and mix well.
5. Mix all ingredients of the topping together. Keep aside.
6. Heat a non stick tawa. Put 1 tbsp of oil on it and then wipe with a potato or onion cut into half.
7. Mix the batter well. Keeping the gas on low flame, pour 1 small karchhi (2 tbsp) of batter on it. Spread the batter a little with the back of the karchhi, keeping it slightly thick. Make small oothapams.

8. After 2 minutes, sprinkle a little topping on it. Pour 2 tsp of oil upon it. Press the topping a little with a potato masher.
9. After the underside is cooked, turn the side carefully.
10. Remove from tawa after the other side also gets cooked and the onions turn a little brown.
11. Serve hot with coconut chutney or tomato ketchup.

Instant Idli

Picture on page 37   *Serves 8*

1 cup suji or rawa, (coarse semolina)
1½ tbsp oil, 1 cup curd (yogurt), a few curry leaves
½ tsp soda-bi-carb (mitha soda), ¾ tsp salt, ½ cup water, approx.

COCONUT CHUTNEY

½ cup freshly grated coconut or desiccated coconut powder (nariyal ka bura)
¼ cup roasted channa or channe ki dal (split gram) - roasted
1 green chilli - chopped, 1 onion - chopped
¾ tsp salt, ¼" piece ginger, 1 cup sour curd (khatti dahi)- approx.

BAGHAR (TADKA) FOR CHUTNEY

1 tbsp oil, 1 tsp sarson (mustard seeds)
1-2 dry red chillies - broken into small pieces, a few curry leaves

1. Heat 1½ tbsp oil in a kadhai. Add suji and mix well. Stir on low heat for 2 minutes till it just starts to change colour. Remove from fire. Add salt. Mix well. Keep aside to cool.
2. Add curd to the suji (suji should cool down) mixture. Mix well with a spoon or a wire whisk. Add soda-bi-carb. Mix very well till smooth.

Keep the batter aside for 10 minutes.

3. Take an idli mould and put 1- 2 drops of oil in each round cup and spread it evenly with your fingers. Put 2 tbsp batter in each cup and put a split cashewnut or curry leaf in each cup.

4. Put a big deep pan filled with 1" high water on fire, to boil. After the water boils, reduce heat. Place the idli mould into the pan of water. Increase heat to medium. Cover the pan with a lid. Steam for 14 minutes undisturbed on medium flame. Insert a knife  in the idli, if it comes out clean it's done. Remove from fire. Remove idlis from the mould after 5 minutes with the help of a knife. Leave them covered in the stand in the pan till serving time.

5. To serve, steam them again for 3-4 minutes till heated properly. Serve hot with coconut chutney given below.

6. For the chutney, grind all ingredients of the chutney in a mixer grinder, adding enough curd to get the right consistency. Keep aside in a bowl. Heat 1 tbsp oil in a small kadhai or pan, add sarson. Wait for ½ a minute, add broken red chillies. Remove from fire, pour baghar immediately into the chutney. Serve with idlis.

LUNCH - Curries & Dry

Has the oil separated from the masala? Is it time to add water or should I bhuno the masala some more... This is where one gets a little confused when making curries.

Sometimes when we do not add too much oil for home cooked meals, the oil actually does not separate and float on the surface. So, when the masala stops sticking to the bottom of the kadhai and starts to collect in the centre as a ball, it is done. The sides of the kadhai or the pan get glossy with oil too. This shows that the oil has separated. Go ahead and add water to get the gravy.

Chhole Bhature

Makes a perfect holiday brunch or lunch! The recipe for bhatura is given later in the bread (roti) section.

Serves 4

PRESSURE COOK TOGETHER

1 cup channa kabuli or saffed chhole (Bengal gram)
¼ tsp soda- bi- carb (mitha soda)
2 moti illaichi (big cardamoms), 1" stick dalchini (cinnamon)
2 tsp tea leaves tied in a muslin cloth or 2 tea bags, 1 tsp salt

MASALA

2 onions - chopped finely
1½ tsp anardaana (pomegranate seeds) - powdered
4 big tomatoes - chopped finely
1" piece ginger - chopped finely, 1 green chilli - chopped finely
1 tsp dhania powder, ½ tsp garam masala
½ tsp red chilli powder or to taste
2 tsp channa masala, 1¼ tsp salt or to taste

1. Soak channas overnight or for 6-8 hours in a pressure cooker. Next morning, discard water. Wash channas with fresh water and add moti illaichi, dalchini, tea leaves, mitha soda, 1 tsp salt and just enough water to cover the channas nicely.
2. Pressure cook all the ingredients together to give one whistle. After the first whistle, keep on low flame for about 15 minutes. Remove from fire. Keep aside.
3. Heat 4 tbsp oil. Add onions. Saute till transparent. Add anardaana powder. Cook stirring till onions turn brown. (Do not burn them).
4. Add chopped tomatoes, ginger and green chill. Stir fry for 5- 6 minutes.
5. Add dhania powder, garam masala and chilli powder. Mash and stir fry tomatoes occasionally for 8-10 minutes or till they turn brown in colour and oil separates.

6. Strain channas, reserving the liquid. Remove tea bag from the boiled channas.

7. Add the strained channas to the onion-tomato masala. Mix well. Stir fry gently for 5-7 minutes.
8. Add channa masala. Add the channa liquid. Check salt and add to taste. Cook for 15-20 minutes on medium heat till the liquid dries up and still a saucy consistency remains.
9. Serve garnished with onion rings, green chillies and tomato wedges.

Matar Paneer

Everyday meals include common dishes like this one, but even the most common ones are made to taste more delicious than the usual. Here seeds of cardamom & cloves do wonders to matar paneer.

Serves 4

200 gms paneer - cut into 1" cubes
1 cup shelled peas (matar)
¼ cup well beaten curd (yogurt) - beat nicely with a wire whisk or fork till smooth
1 tsp dhania (coriander) powder
½ tsp red chilli powder
¼ tsp amchoor, ¼ tsp garam masala, 4-5 tbsp oil

ONION-TOMATO PASTE
2 onions, 3 tomatoes
1" piece ginger, 2 cloves (laung)
seeds of 1 moti illaichi (brown cardamoms)

1. Grind all ingredients of onion-tomato paste in a mixer.

2. Heat 4- 5 tbsp oil in a kadhai. Add the onion - tomato paste. Cook covered on high flame for about 5 minutes till dry. Remove cover and cook, stirring frequently for 5-7 minutes till very thick and absolutely dry.

3. Add dhania powder, red chilli powder, amchoor and garam masala. Reduce heat and cook for 5 minutes more till oil separates. The masala should be dry and look glossy because the oil separates which makes the masala as well as the sides of the kadhai turn glossy.

4. Beat curd with a wire whisk or fork till very smooth.

5. Add well beaten curd to the masala, stir continuously for about 3-4 minutes, till oil separates again and the masala turns to a bright red colour.

6. Add enough water, about 2½ cups water, to get a thick gravy. Add salt to taste, about 1 tsp salt. Cover and cook the gravy for about 5 minutes on low heat till oil separates and comes to the surface.

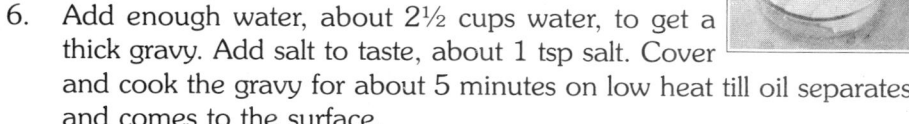

7. Add peas. Cook covered till peas are done.

8. Add paneer and ¼ tsp garam masala. Cook on low heat for 3-4 minutes till paneer gets soft. Serve hot.

Rajmah

Picture on back cover   *Serves 6*

1½ cups rajmah (red kidney beans) - soaked overnight
2½ tsp salt or to taste
5 tbsp oil
1 tej patta (bay leaf), 1 moti illaichi (black cardamom), 2 laung (cloves)
¼ tsp haldi, 3 tsp dhania powder, ¼ tsp amchoor
½ tsp garam masala, 1 tsp red chilli powder, or to taste
3 tomatoes - pureed in a grinder
½ cup curd - beaten well till smooth
2 tbsp chopped coriander

ONION PASTE
2 onions, 1" piece ginger, 6-8 flakes garlic

1. Drain the soaked rajmah. Wash well with fresh water. Pressure cook rajmah and salt with about 10 cups water to give one whistle. Keep on low flame for 15 minutes. Remove from fire.

2. Grind onion, ginger and garlic to a paste.
3. Heat 5 tbsp oil in a heavy bottomed kadhai. Add tej patta, moti illaichi and laung. Wait for 1 minute.
4. Add onion paste. Stir fry till golden brown on medium heat.
5. Reduce heat. Add haldi, dhania powder, amchoor, garam masala and red chilli powder. Stir for a few seconds.
6. Add tomatoes pureed in a mixer. Cook till tomatoes turn dry and oil separates.

7. Reduce heat. Add beaten curd, stirring continuously on low flame till the masala turns red again and oil separates.
8. Strain and add the rajmahs, keeping the water aside. Stir fry on medium flame for 2-3 minutes, mashing occasionally.
9. Add the water of the rajmahs and close the pressure cooker. Pressure cook again for 8-10 minutes on low flame after the first whistle. Remove from fire. Add freshly chopped coriander leaves. Serve hot with chappatis or boiled rice.

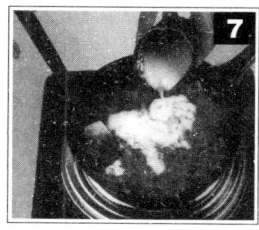

Sambar

Serve with boiled rice, papad and some salad.

Picture on facing page   Serves 6

1 cup arhar ki dal (red gram lentils), 2 tsp salt, or to taste
6-8 french beans - cut into 1" long pieces
a 2" square piece of kaddu (pumpkin) or ghiya (bottle gourd) - cut into ½" pieces
2-3 tbsp oil
¼ tsp hing powder or 2 grains of hing
a pinch of methi dana (fenugreek seeds)
½ tsp jeera (cumin seeds), ½ tsp sarson (mustard seeds)
2 dry, red chillies - broken into small pieces
2 tbsp curry leaves, 2 onions - cut into thin slices
2 tbsp sambar powder, a lemon sized ball of imli (tamarind)

TEMPERING (BAGHAR)
1 tsp desi ghee
a few curry leaves, ¼ tsp red chilli powder

Instant Idli : Recipe on page 26 ➢

1. Pressure cook dal with 6 cups of water and salt to give 3 whistles. Keep on low heat for 5 minutes. Remove from fire.
2. Wash imli and boil with 1 cup water. After it cools, extract juice. Add 1 more cup water to the left over imli and extract more juice.
3. Heat oil in a heavy bottomed kadhai. Reduce flame. Add hing and methi dana.
4. After a few seconds, add jeera, sarson and dry red chilli.
5. When it splutters after 1 minute, add some curry leaves.
6. Add onions. Fry till onions turn light brown.
7. Add vegetables - french beans & pumpkin or gourd. Stir for 2 minutes.
8. Reduce heat. Add sambar powder. Bhuno for 1 minute on low heat.
9. Add imli juice. Boil. Simmer for 1-2 minutes.
10. Add the cooked dal. Simmer for 10-15 minutes till everything blends well together. Remove from fire.
11. At serving time, heat the sambar. For the baghar, heat 1 tsp desi ghee in a small pan. Shut off the flame. Add a few curry leaves and a pinch of red chilli powder.
12. Add the baghar to the hot sambar. Mix and serve.

◄ *Masala Pooda : Recipe on page 22*

Gobhi Aloo

Serves 4

1 medium cauliflower (350-400 gm) - cut into medium florets
1-2 potatoes - cut into 1" pieces
2 onions - chopped
1" piece ginger - chopped finely
2 tomatoes - chopped
4 tbsp oil
1¼ tsp salt, ½ tsp haldi
2 tsp dhania powder
½ tsp garam masala
½ tsp amchoor powder
½ tsp red chilli powder
2 tbsp chopped coriander
1-2 green chillies - keep whole

1. Wash gobhi. Wipe dry on a kitchen towel.
2. Heat oil. Add onions and ginger. Cook till light brown.
3. Add salt and haldi.
4. Add tomatoes and stir for 3-4 minutes.
5. Add dhania powder, garam masala, amchoor and red chilli powder.
6. Add gobhi and aloo to the masala. Mix well.
7. Cover with a tight fitting lid and cook on low heat till aloo gets cooked for about 7-8 minutes.
8. Remove cover and add green chillies. Bhuno the gobhi on medium flame till the gobhi looks done.
9. Serve garnished with coriander.

Note: Before adding gobhi to the masala, remember to wipe dry with a cloth. If even a little water is added with the gobhi, it turns mushy.

Gajar Matar

Gajar matar tastes best with less masalas and slightly less salt. The sweetness of the carrots is what one enjoys!

Serves 4

3 large carrots - cut into ¼" cubes (2 cups chopped)
1½ cups shelled peas (matar)
2 tsp finely chopped ginger
3-4 tbsp finely chopped coriander
2 tbsp oil
½ tsp jeera
¾ tsp salt, ¼ tsp haldi
¼ tsp red chilli powder
¼ tsp pepper powder
1 tsp lemon juice

1. Wash chopped carrots and peas and keep aside.
2. Heat oil in a heavy bottomed kadhai. Reduce heat. Add jeera. Let it turn golden.
3. Add salt, haldi and red chilli powder.
4. Add ginger and stir.
5. Add carrots and peas. Stir fry for 1-2 minutes on low flame.
6. Cover and cook on low flame, for about 10 minutes, till peas are done. Do not overcook the vegetable as it loses its colourful look.
7. Add coriander. Add pepper powder and lemon juice. Uncover and stir fry for 2-3 minutes. Serve hot.

Kale Chane Rasse Waale

An extremely healthy curry - full of Iron and proteins.
Tastes delicious with jeera rice.

Picture on page 48   *Servings 4*

1½ cups kale channe - soaked overnight in water
1½ tsp salt or to taste, 2 onions
¼ tsp haldi, 2 tsp dhania powder, ½ tsp amchoor
½ tsp garam masala, ½ tsp chilli powder, or to taste
1 tsp salt, 1 tsp channa masala, 2 laung (cloves)
2 moti illaichi (black cardamoms), 2-3 cinnamon (dalchini) sticks

PASTE
3 tomatoes, 2 onions, 6-8 flakes garlic, 1" piece ginger

1. Drain the channas. Wash well. Pressure cook kale channe and 1½ tsp salt with about 4 cups water to give 4 whistles. Keep on low flame for 20 minutes. Remove from fire.

2. Grind onion, tomato, ginger and garlic to a paste in a mixer.

3. Heat 4 tbsp oil in a heavy bottomed kadhai. Add dalchini, moti illaichi and laung. Wait for 1 minute.

4. Add paste and stir fry for about 10 minutes, till golden brown and dry.

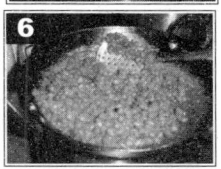

5. Reduce heat. Add haldi, dhania powder, amchoor, garam masala and red chilli powder, salt and channa masala. Stir for a few seconds.

6. Strain the kale channe, keeping (reserving) the water aside. Stir fry on medium flame for 2-3 minutes, mashing occasionally.

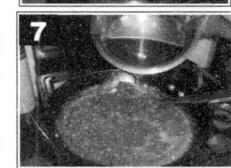

7. Add about 3 cups of the reserved water of the kale channe.

8. Give 2-3 boils and keep on low flame for 15-20 minutes. Check salt.

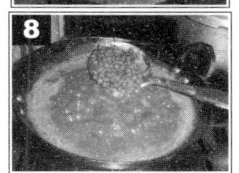

9. Remove from fire. Serve hot with chappatis or boiled rice.

Saffed Chhole-Rasse Waale

It is always advisable to throw the water in which the channas have been soaked. Using the same water can cause indigestion!

Picture on facing page   *Serves 4*

1 cup saffed chhole (kabuli channe) - soak overnight in water
1 tsp salt

OTHER INGREDIENTS
5 tbsp oil
¾ tsp jeera (cumin seeds)
2 onions - finely chopped
1 tsp ginger paste, 1 tsp garlic paste
½ tsp garam masala, ½ tsp red chilli powder
2 tsp dhania powder
¼ tsp haldi (turmeric powder), 1 tsp chaana masala
3 tomatoes - finely chopped
1 tbsp kasoori methi (dry fenugreek leaves), optional

1. Drain the water from the soaked channas. To boil channas, put channas, 4 cups fresh water and 1 tsp salt in a pressure cooker. Give two whistles and keep on low flame for 15-20 minutes. Remove from fire and let the pressure drop by itself. Strain, **reserving the water**. Keep aside.
2. Heat 5 tbsp oil in a kadhai, add jeera, let it turn golden.
3. Add chopped onions. Cook till golden brown.
4. Add ginger and garlic paste. Stir till onions turn a rich brown in colour.
5. Reduce heat. Add garam masala, red chilli powder, dhania powder, haldi, channa masala. Mix well.
6. Add chopped tomatoes and kasoori methi. Cook for about 7-8 minutes, till oil separates and the tomatoes blend very well with the masala.
7. Add boiled chhole. Mix well and cook for 6-7 minutes.
8. Add the reserved water. Give 2 boils and cook covered on low heat for 10 minutes. Serve hot with boiled rice.

◁ *Kale Chane Rasse Waale : Recipe on page 44*
◁ *Simla Mirch Aloo : Recipe on page 50*

Simla Mirch Aloo

A quick dry vegetable, strongly flavoured with carom seeds.

Picture on page 48   *Serves 4*

2 large potatoes - cut into thin long fingers
3 capsicums - cut into thin long fingers
1 tsp lemon juice
2 tbsp oil
1 tsp ajwain (carom seeds)
5-6 flakes garlic crushed or 1 tsp finely chopped ginger
3 tomatoes (250 gm) - grind to a puree in a mixer
¼ tsp haldi, 2 tsp dhania powder
1 tsp salt, ½ tsp red chilli powder
½ tsp garam masala
1 tbsp tomato ketchup

1. Cut potatoes into round slices first. Cut each slice into thin fingers like potato chips. Soak fingers in cold water to which 1 tsp salt and 1 tsp lemon juice has been added. Soak for 10 minutes. Drain and wipe dry.

2. Deep fry all potato fingers together in oil on medium flame till golden brown and cooked. Keep aside.

3. Heat 2 tbsp oil. Add ajwain. Wait for a minute.

4. Add garlic or ginger. Let it change colour.

5. Add fresh tomato puree. Stir for 5-6 minutes till dry.

6. Add all masalas - haldi, dhania, salt, red chilli and garam masala. Stir till oil separates.

7. Add tomato ketchup. Add 2 tbsp water. Mix.

8. Add capsicums. Mix. Keep aside till serving time.

9. To serve, add the fried potatoes. Stir to mix well. Serve hot.

Note: Make the potato chips well browned and crisp.

Matar Aloo

Picture on page 68   *Serves 4*

3 potatoes, 1 cup boiled or frozen peas (matar)
4 tbsp oil, 1 tsp jeera (cumin seeds)
1 large onion - chopped very finely
1 tsp salt, or to taste, ¼ tsp haldi (turmeric powder)
½ tsp garam masala, ½ tsp red chilli powder, ½ tsp amchoor
2 -3 green chillies - whole, 2-3 tbsp chopped coriander
2 tsp lemon juice
1 tsp til (sesame seeds) - optional

1. Put potatoes in a deep pan (patila), cover them with water. Bring to a boil. Cook covered on low heat for 7-8 minutes till soft. They should feel soft when a knife is inserted. Do not over cook. (You may also pressure cook the potatoes to give one whistle. For a quicker subzi, microwave the potatoes if you wish — 4 potatoes would take about 4 minutes on full power).

2. Peel and cut each potato into 4 equal pieces.
3. Heat oil in a non stick pan or kadhai. Reduce heat. Add jeera. Wait till the jeera starts changing colour.
4. Add chopped onions. Stir until onions turn light brown.

5. Add salt, haldi, garam masala, red chilli powder and amchoor. Mix.
6. Add whole green chillies and fresh coriander. Cook for 1 minute.
7. Add 2-3 tbsp water. Mix.
8. Add the potatoes. Stir-fry gently for about 5-6 minutes on low heat, taking care not to break the potatoes. Keep the potatoes spread out in the kadhai/pan to get crisp potatoes.
9. Finally add peas. Mix gently. Cook for 2 minutes stirring occasionally. Add lemon juice and mix well. Remove from fire. Serve hot.
10. If you like, dry roast sesame seeds on a tawa (griddle) for 2 minutes on low heat till golden. Remove from tawa and top the matar above with sesame seeds. Serve.

DINNER
Curries & Dry

Kati Arbi

Serves 4   *Picture on page 58*

½ kg arbi (colocassia)
1 tsp ajwain, 1 tsp haldi, 1¼ tsp dhania powder
½ tsp garam masala, 1 tsp salt

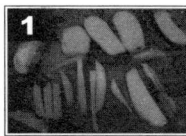

1. Wash and peel arbi. Cut each lengthwise into 2 pieces. Cut each piece into thin fingers.
2. Heat 5 tbsp oil in a big kadhai or a pan. Add ajwain and wait for 1 minute.

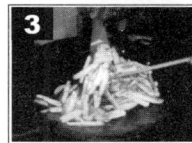

3. Add arbi fingers, haldi, dhania powder, garam masala and salt. Mix well.
4. Cook covered on low heat for 8-10 minutes, keeping them spaced out. Cook till almost done but not mushy.
5. Cook uncovered on high heat for 8-10 minutes or till crisp. Serve hot.

Channe ki Dal with Ghiya

Picture on facing page   *Serves 4*

1 cup channe ki dal (split gram)
½ small ghiya (bottle gourd) - peeled & chopped (1 cup)
1½ tsp salt, ½ tsp haldi (turmeric powder), 2 tsp desi ghee or oil
½ tsp red chilli powder

TADKA
3-4 tbsp ghee or oil
½ tsp jeera (cumin seeds)
1 tsp chopped ginger
1 onion - chopped finely
2 tomatoes - chopped finely
½ tsp red chilli powder
½ tsp garam masala
½ tsp dhania (coriander) powder
¼ tsp amchoor (dried mango powder)
1 green chilli - slit lengthwise into four pieces

1. Pick, clean and wash dal.
2. Mix dal, ghiya, salt, haldi, desi ghee, red chilli powder and 4 cups water in a pressure cooker.
3. Pressure cook for 5 minutes on low flame after the first whistle. Remove from fire.
4. For the tadka, heat oil or ghee, reduce heat. Add jeera. When it turns golden, add ginger. Stir for 1 minute. Add onions.
5. Cook till onions turn brown. Do not undercook the onions. Brown them, stirring continuously.
6. Add tomatoes. Cook for 2-3 minutes on low flame.
7. Add dhania powder, amchoor and garam masala. Cook for ½ minute.
8. Remove from fire. Add the green chillies and red chilli powder. Mix well.
9. Pour over the hot dal. Mix gently.

◁ *Kati Arbi : Recipe on page 55*

Paneer Makhani

Serves 4

250 gm paneer - cut into 1" cubes, 6 (500 gm) tomatoes - each cut into 4 pieces
2 tbsp desi ghee or butter, 2 tbsp oil
4-5 flakes garlic and 1" piece ginger - ground to a paste
(1½ tsp ginger-garlic paste)
1 tbsp kasoori methi (dry fenugreek leaves), 1 tsp tomato ketchup
½ tsp jeera (cumin seeds), 2 tsp dhania powder, ½ tsp garam masala
1 tsp salt, or to taste, ½ tsp red chilli powder, preferably degi mirch
½-1 cup milk, approx., ½ cup water
½ cup cream (optional), 3 tbsp cashewnuts (kaju)

1. Soak kaju in a ½ cup warm water for 10-15 minutes. Drain the water.
2. Grind kajus in a small mixer to a very smooth paste using about 4-5 tbsp water.
3. Boil tomatoes in ½ cup water. Cover and cook on low heat for 4-5 minutes till tomatoes turn soft. Remove from fire and cool. Grind the tomatoes alongwith the water to a smooth puree.
4. Heat 2 tbsp oil and 2 tbsp ghee or butter in a kadhai. Reduce heat.

Add jeera. When it turns golden, add ginger-garlic paste.

5. When paste starts to change colour, add the above tomato puree. Cook till puree turns dry.
6. Add kasoori methi and tomato ketchup.
7. Add masalas - dhania powder, garam masala, salt and red chilli powder. Mix well for a few seconds. Cook till oil separates and the masala turns glossy.
8. Add cashew paste. Mix well for 2 minutes.

9. Add water. Boil. Simmer on low heat for 4-5 minutes. Remove from fire. Keep aside to cool for about 5 minutes.
10. Add enough milk to the cold masala to get a thick curry, mix gently. (Remember to add milk only after the masala is no longer hot, to prevent the milk from curdling. After adding milk, heat curry on low heat).
11. Add the paneer cubes. Keep aside till serving time.
12. To serve heat on low flame, stirring continuously till just about to boil.
13. Add cream, keeping the heat very low and stirring gently. Remove from fire immediately and transfer to a serving dish. Swirl 1 tbsp cream over the hot paneer in the dish. Serve immediately.

Koftas in Green Gravy

Picture on page 103   *Serves 4*

KOFTA

1 cup cooked rice, 200 gm paneer - grated (2 cups)
¼ tsp baking powder, ½ tsp salt, ½ tsp pepper, ½ tsp red chilli powder
4 tbsp grated paneer, a pinch of haldi, salt, 1 tsp chopped peanuts or almonds

GRAVY

1 bunch of paalak (600 gm), 1 green chilli - chopped
2 tomatoes - pureed in a mixer or 6 tbsp readymade tomato puree

GRIND TO A PASTE

2 onions, 8-10 flakes of garlic, 1" piece of ginger
1½ tbsp dhania powder, ½ tsp red chilli powder
1 tsp garam masala, ½ tsp haldi, 1½ tsp salt, or to taste

1. For the koftas, mix together cooked rice, 200 gms paneer, baking powder, salt, pepper and red chilli powder. Mix well. Keep aside.
2. Mix 4 tbsp grated paneer with haldi, salt and chopped peanuts or almonds. Make tiny balls of this yellow mixture.
3. Make lemon sized balls of the rice-paneer mixture. Flatten and place

a yellow ball in the centre. Cover the yellow ball with the sides of the white mixture to form a ball again with the rice paneer mixture.

4. Fry koftas in medium hot oil, one at a time till golden. Keep aside.
5. For the gravy, break spinach leaves. Wash in several changes of water. To boil spinach, put ½ cup water in a pan. Add ¼ tsp sugar. Add spinach leaves. Boil for 2-3 minutes on low heat without covering. Remove from fire. Cool. Grind the cooked spinach along with a fresh green chilli to a green puree. Keep aside.
6. Grind all ingredients of paste to a smooth paste in a mixer.
7. Heat 3 tbsp oil in a kadhai. Add onion paste. Stir till it turns golden.
8. Add paalak paste and bhuno for 5-7 minutes.
9. Add tomato paste or puree. Cook for 2-3 minutes.
10. Add about 1½ cups of water to get the consistency of the gravy. Boil. Simmer on low heat for 5-7 minutes. Keep gravy aside.
11. To serve, heat the gravy. Add koftas and keep on low heat for 1-2 minutes till the koftas are heated through. Transfer to a serving dish. Cut each into 2 pieces to expose the yellow portion. Serve hot.

Note: If you have a microwave, cut the koftas into 2 pieces and arrange in a dish with palak gravy. Microwave and serve hot.

Mixed Dal

Picture on cover   *Serves 4*

¼ cup channa dal (yellow gram dal), ¼ cup moong chilka (green split dal)
¼ cup dhuli masoor (orange dal), ¼ cup dhuli urad (whitish dal)

TADKA

1½ tsp panch phoran (a combination of 5 seeds - sarson, kalaunji, jeera, methi daana, saunf)

4-5 flakes garlic - crushed, 1" piece ginger - chopped finely

1 tomato - chopped finely, ½ tsp each of dhania & garam masala

¼ tsp amchoor, 1 tbsp chopped coriander

1. Wash all dals together in a pressure cooker. Add 3½ cups water, 1 tsp salt and 1/3 tsp haldi. Pressure cook to give 1 whistle and then keep on low flame for 4 min. Remove from fire. Let pressure drop by itself.
2. Heat 3 tbsp oil. Add panch phoran (sarson, kalaunji, jeera, methi daana, saunf).
3. When methi dana turns golden, add garlic and ginger. Stir.
4. Add tomatoes. Add ½ tsp dhania, ½ tsp garam masala and ¼ tsp amchoor. Cook for 3-4 minutes till tomatoes are well blended.
5. Pour on the cooked dal. Garnish with chopped coriander.

Kati Bhindi

The regular okra, looks more appetizing if cut lengthwise.

Serves 3-4

300 gm bhindi (okra) - cut into 4 pieces lengthwise
3 tbsp oil, 1 onion - sliced
¾ tsp salt
¼ red chilli powder
1 tsp dhania powder
½ tsp garam masala
½ tsp haldi
½ tsp amchoor

1. Wash and slice of ¼" from the base of each bhindi. Keep the pointed end as it is. Cut each bhindi into 4 pieces lengthwise. Keep aside.
2. Heat oil in a kadhai. Add onions and stir till light golden.
3. Add all the masalas except salt. Mix and add bhindi. Cook for 15 minutes keeping the bhindi spread out in the kadhai.
4. Sprinkle salt. Mix well. Add more masalas if needed. Serve.

Baingan ka Bharta

Picture on facing page   *Serves 3-4*

1 medium baingan (brinjal) of round variety (350 gm)
2 onions - chopped finely
2 tomatoes - pureed in a mixer
1 tomato - chopped finely
½" piece ginger - chopped finely
1 green chilli - chopped
2 tsp dhania (coriander) powder
¼ tsp haldi
½ tsp garam masala
½ tsp degi mirch or red chilli powder
1 tsp salt

1. Rub 1 tsp oil all over the baingan and roast over a gas flame until the skin gets charred and starts to peel off and flesh is soft.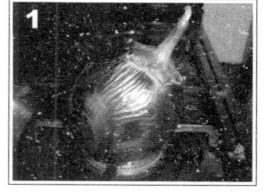

2. Remove the charred skin from the brinjal. Mash the flesh with a fork and keep pulp aside. If the seeds are too big and hard, discard them.

3. In a kadhai, heat 3-4 tbsp oil. Add onions, ginger and green chilli. Cook till onions turn golden brown.

4. Add dhania, haldi, garam masala and degi mirch. Cook for 2 minutes.

5. Add mashed brinjal and bhuno for 10 minutes on medium heat.

6. Add chopped tomato, tomato puree and 1 tsp salt. Mix well. Cook for 7-8 minutes. Serve hot.

◁ *Matar Aloo : Recipe on page 52*

Bharwaan Karele

Serves 4-6

½ kg small karelas (bitter gourd) - peeled, slit & deseeded
1 tsp salt
2 tbsp (a lemon sized ball) imli (tamarind)
3 tbsp plus 3 tbsp (6 tbsp) oil
1 tsp saunf and 1 tsp jeera
3 onions - chopped very finely
½ tsp salt, ½ tsp chilli powder
2 tsp dhania (coriander) powder, ¼ tsp haldi
1 tsp amchoor, a pinch of sugar
6-8 small baby onions, optional - peel and give 2 cross cuts halfway
some chaat masala

1. Boil 8 cups water with 2 tsp salt. Add peeled and deseeded karelas. Boil on medium heat for 7-10 minutes or till soft. Strain. Keep aside.
2. Heat 3 tbsp oil in a pan. Add saunf and jeera and stir for a few seconds till jeera turns golden brown.
3. Add onions and cook till light golden in colour.
4. Add salt, red chilli powder and dhania powder. Add the amchoor and sugar. Cook till dry. Remove from heat and keep the filling aside to cool.
5. Squeeze the karelas lightly. Fill the boiled karela with the prepared onion mixture. Tie with a thread, so that the filling does not come out while cooking.
6. Heat the remaining 3 tbsp oil in a big, heavy bottomed pan or kadhai. Place each karela carefully in oil. Turn a little to coat with oil. Then shift to the side. Add all the karelas. Keep them side by side and not overlapping each other. Cook on medium heat for 10-15 minutes stirring in-between till karelas turn golden brown on all sides.
7. Add whole onions and cook further for 5 minutes. Sprinkle chaat masala. Remove from fire and serve hot.

Dal Makhani

Originally the dal was cooked by leaving it overnight on the burning coal angithis. The longer the dal simmered, the better it tasted.

Serves 4-5

1 cup urad saboot (kali dal) - soak atleast for 3 hrs, or preferably overnight
2 tbsp desi ghee, 1½ tsp salt, 5 cups of water, 1 cup ready made tomato puree
a pinch or ¼ tsp jaiphal powder (optional), ½ tsp garam masala
1½ tbsp kasoori methi (dry fenugreek leaves)
2-3 tbsp butter, preferably white

GRIND TO A PASTE
2 dry, whole red chillies,
preferably Kashmiri red chillies - deseeded & soaked for 10 min & then drained
1" piece ginger, 6-8 flakes garlic

ADD LATER
½ cup milk mixed with ½ cup cream

1. Wash the dal and soak in warm water for atleast 3 hours or preferably overnight.
2. Drain water. Wash several times in fresh water, rubbing well, till the water no longer remains black.
3. Pressure cook dal with 5 cups water, 2 tbsp ghee, salt and ginger-garlic-chilli paste. After the first whistle, keep on low flame for 30 minutes. Remove from fire.
4. After the pressure drops, mash the hot dal a little with a karchhi. Keep aside.

5. To the dal in the cooker, add tomato puree, kasoori methi, garam masala and jaiphal powder.
6. Add butter. Simmer on medium flame for 20 minutes, stirring dal occasionally. Remove from fire. Keep aside to cool till the time of serving.
7. At the time of serving, add milk mixed with cream to the dal. Keep dal on fire and bring to a boil on low heat, stirring constantly. Mix very well with a karchhi. Simmer for 2 minutes more, to get the right colour and smoothness. Remove from fire. Serve.

Special Mixed Subzi

Picture on cover   *Serves 4*

2 tbsp oil, ½ tsp jeera, ½ tsp sarson, ½ tsp kalonji, ¼ tsp methi daana
15-20 curry leaves
2 onions - cut into rings, ¼ tsp haldi

MIX TOGETHER

¾ cup readymade tomato puree
2 tsp tomato ketchup
2 tsp ginger-garlic paste or 2 tsp ginger-garlic - finely chopped
½ tsp red chilli powder, ½ tsp amchoor powder, 1 tsp dhania powder, 1 tsp salt

VEGETABLES

1 carrot - cut diagonally into thin slices
10-12 french beans - sliced diagonally into 1" pieces
8-10 small florets (pieces) of cauliflower
1 green capsicum - deseed and cut into thin fingers
½ cup shelled peas (matar) - boiled
1 long, firm tomato - cut into 4 and then cut into thin long pieces

1. Boil 4 cups water with 1 tsp salt and ½ tsp sugar. Add sliced carrots and beans after the water boils. Boil for 2 minutes till crisp-tender. Strain. Refresh in cold water.
2. Mix together - tomato puree, tomato ketchup, ginger, garlic, red chilli powder, dhania powder, amchoor and salt in a bowl. Keep aside.
3. Collect together - jeera, sarson, kalonji and methi dana. Keep aside. Heat 2 tbsp oil in a kadhai. Add the collected ingredients. When jeera turns golden, reduce heat and add curry leaves and stir for a few seconds.
4. Add onions and cook till golden. Add haldi. Mix.
5. Add the tomato puree mixed with dry masalas and stir on medium heat for 2 minutes.
6. Add carrot, cauliflower and beans. Stir for 3-4 minutes.
7. Add the capsicum, peas and tomato. Stir till well blended. Remove from fire.
8. Transfer to a serving dish. Serve hot.

Paalak Paneer

Picture on facing page   *Serves 4*

½ kg paalak (spinach), choose a bundle with smaller leaves
1 moti illaichi (brown cardamom), 2-3 laung (cloves)
3-4 saboot kali mirch (peppercorns), 3 onions - chopped,
1" piece ginger - chopped, 4-6 flakes garlic - chopped, 1 green chilli - chopped
1 tbsp kasoori methi (dried fenugreek leaves), ¾ tsp garam masala
½ tsp red chilli powder, ¼ tsp amchoor, 1¼ tsp salt, or to taste
2 tomatoes - chopped, 100 gms paneer (cottage cheese) - cut into 1" cubes

BAGHAR (TEMPERING)
1 tbsp desi ghee or butter, 1" piece ginger - cut into thin long pieces (juliennes)
1 green chilli - slit into long pieces, ½ tsp red chilli powder

1. Break paalak leaves into small pieces. Discard stalks. Wash leaves in plenty of water. Keep aside to drain.
2. Heat 3 tbsp oil in a kadhai. Add moti illaichi, laung & saboot kali mirch.
3. Add onions and cook till light brown.
4. Add ginger, garlic and green chillies. Stir on low flame for 1 minute. Add kasoori methi.

5. Add garam masala, red chilli powder, amchoor and salt. Stir on low flame for 1 minute.

6. Add chopped tomatoes. Cook for 3-4 minutes, till well blended.

7. Add spinach and cook uncovered for 10-12 minutes on low flame. Remove from fire. Cool.

8. Blend the cooled mixture along with ½ cup water, just for a few seconds, to a coarse paste. Do not grind it too finely.

9. Boil 1 cup water and add the spinach paste to it. Simmer, uncovered for 4-5 minutes.

10. Mix paneer pieces in the cooked spinach. Give it one boil. Simmer for 2-3 minutes till paneer turns soft. Transfer to a serving dish.

11. Heat 1 tbsp desi ghee or butter. Add ginger and green chilli. Remove from fire. Add red chilli powder and pour ghee on the hot paalak. Mix lightly. Serve.

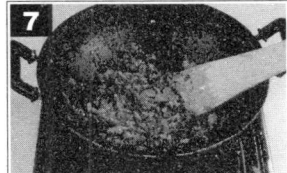

◁ *Kadhai Babycorns : Recipe on page 80*

Kadhai Babycorns

Picture on page 78   *Serves 4*

200 gm baby corns (20 pieces approx.)
juice of ½ lemon
2 capsicums - cut into thin fingers
1-2 dry red chillies - deseeded
1½ tsp saboot dhania (coriander seeds)
a pinch of methi daana (fenugreek seeds)
1" piece ginger and 6- 8 flakes of garlic - crushed to a paste (2 tsp paste)
2 onions - chopped, 4 tomatoes
1 tbsp kasoori methi (dry fenugreek leaves)
¼ tsp haldi, ½ tsp garam masala
½ tsp amchoor, 1¼ tsp salt, or to taste
2 tbsp chopped coriander
½" piece ginger - cut into match sticks or shredded on the grater (1 tsp)

1. Boil 5 cups water. Add whole tomatoes, 1 tsp salt, 1 tbsp lemon juice and babycorn. Boil them for 2 minutes. Remove from fire. Strain through a sieve (channi). Separate the tomatoes and keep aside. Put babycorn under running water (refresh). Let them cool down. Cut into 2 pieces lengthwise, if thick or keep whole. Peel the blanched tomatoes and chop finely.

2. Warm red chillies and dhania saboot on a tawa, till slightly crisp and dry, for about 30 seconds.

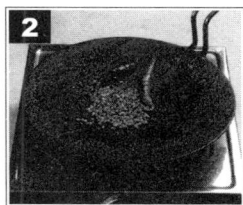

3. Roughly grind red chillies and saboot dhania to a rough powder in a small spice grinder.

4. Heat 2 tbsp oil in a pan or kadhai and add the boiled baby corns. Bhuno for 4-5 minutes till they start turning brown. Keep them spaced out while bhunoing and let them not overlap each other. Add the capsicum strips and stir fry for 2 minutes. Remove from pan/kadhai and keep aside.

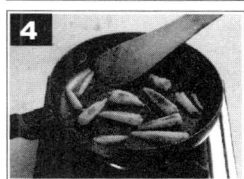

5. Heat 3 tbsp oil in a kadhai. Remove from fire. Add a pinch of methi daana. Let it turn golden brown.

Contd...

6. Return to fire. Add onion. Cook till onions turn golden brown.
7. Add ginger- garlic paste. Mix well.
8. Add roasted dhania-red chilli powder. Stir for 30 seconds.
9. Add peeled and chopped tomatoes. Stir for 4-5 minutes on low heat till dry.
10. Add haldi, garam masala, amchoor, salt and kasoori methi.
11. Add fresh coriander. Mix well till oil separates. Add ½ cup water. Let it boil. Remove from fire and keep aside till serving time.
12. At the time of serving, add baby corns and capsicum. Cook for 2-3 minutes.

Rice, Roti and Raitas

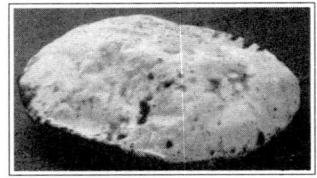

Chappati or Phulka

Serves 4

2 cups atta (whole wheat flour), ½ cup water - approx., 2 tsp ghee - optional

1. Sift atta into a flat basin (parat). Add water gradually, and keep collecting the atta together till it can bind together. Form a ball of the dough. Now punch it down with your knuckles or hands to knead it to a smooth and soft dough. Knead for about 2-3 minutes to make it smooth. Wrap the dough in a thick damp cloth and keep aside in the same basin. Cover the basin and keep aside for atleast 30 minutes.
2. Knead the dough again for 2-3 minutes, when you start making the chapatis.

3. To make chapatis, make balls, slightly smaller than the size of a lemon.
4. Heat the tawa (griddle) on fire.
5. Roll balls into fairly thin rounds, about 5-6" in diameter.
6. Place the chapati on the hot griddle and reduce the flame. Cook the chapati on moderate heat throughout.
7. Turn over when tiny bubbles appear on the surface. Cook till brown spots are formed on the under surface.
8. Turn over and press lightly on the sides with a folded cloth till the chapati is puffed or bloated. Many find it more comfortable to remove the chapati from tawa and puff up the roti on direct flame with the help of tongs. But such rotis do not keep well. They are good if served immediately.

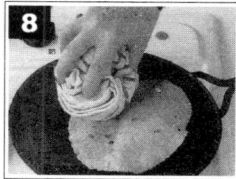

Cracked and Hard Roti...

If you make roti from a freshly kneaded dough, they are bound to be hard. Always remember to make dough and keep it covered for atleast 30 minutes for gluten formation which gives elasticity to the dough and makes rotis soft.

Saada Parantha

Makes 7-8

2½ cups atta (whole wheat flour)
1 cup water (approx.)
½ tsp salt, ½ tsp red chilli powder, ½ tsp ajwain (carom seeds)
2-3 tbsp ghee

1. Mix atta, salt , red chilli powder and ajwain in a shallow bowl (paraat). Add water gradually, and keep collecting the atta together till it can bind together. Form a ball of the dough. Now punch it down with your knuckles or hands to knead it to a smooth and soft dough. Knead for about 2-3 minutes to make it smooth. Wet a thick cloth napkin and squeeze well. Wrap the dough in the damp cloth and cover the paraat. Keep aside for atleast 30 minutes.
2. Divide the dough into big lemon sized balls. Flatten each ball, roll out each into a round of 5" diameter.

3. Spread 1 tsp of ghee. Sprinkle a teaspoon of dry flour on the ghee.
4. Make a slit, starting from centre to the end.
5. Start rolling from the slit, to form an even cone.
6. Hold the cone upright. Press a little from the centre of the cone to flatten slightly.
7. Coat in dry flour and roll out, to a diameter of 5", applying pressure only at the centre while rolling, and not on the sides. If too much pressure is applied on the sides, the parantha does not turn flaky.
8. Place a tawa on fire on medium heat. Put the parantha on the hot tawa. Turn side after a minute. Put ghee around the edges and spread some on top. Turn again and fry till golden. Remove on a cloth napkin and crush the parantha lightly along with the cloth so that the layers open up slightly.

Quick Peethi Poori

Raw dal is ground to a paste and smeared on the poori to make it crisp & tasty.

Makes 12

1 cup atta (whole wheat flour)
½ tsp salt
1 tsp oil or melted ghee
¼ cup urad dal - soaked for 2 hours and coarsely ground to get peethi
or
½ cup ready made urad dal ki peethi
½ tsp salt
1 tsp kuti laal mirch (red chilli flakes)
¼ tsp ajwain (carom seeds)

1. Sift flour and ½ tsp salt together. Add in melted ghee or oil.
2. Knead to a little stiff dough with about ¾ cup water. Cover and mix well with the fingers. Set aside.
3. Mix dal ki peethi with ½ tsp salt, 1 tsp kuti laal mirch and ¼ tsp ajwain.
4. Divide dough into small balls and roll out the balls into small poories.
5. Spread 1 tsp full peethi on the rolled out poori with the spoon.
6. Heat oil, drop the rolled poories gently into it with the peethi side down in the oil, so that the dal gets cooked in the hot oil.
7. Press the sides of the poori with a perforated frying spoon (chhara) and make the poori swell up. Turn. Fry till golden brown. Drain on paper napkin.

Note: The peethi can be stuffed inside the poori also, but the above method is quicker!

Vegetable Pullao

Serves 4

1 cup uncooked rice
3 tbsp oil
1 tsp jeera (cumin seeds)
2-3 laung (cloves), 2 moti illaichi (black cardamom)
1 small stick dalchini (cinnamon), 1 tej patta (bay leaf)
2 onions - thinly sliced
1½ tsp salt or to taste
½ cup shelled peas (matar)
1 small carrot - cut into small pieces
6-8 french beans - cut into small pieces

1. Wash the rice and strain. Keep in the strainer (channi) for 30 minutes.
2. Heat oil in a heavy bottomed pan. Reduce flame. Add jeera, dalchini, tej patta, laung and moti illaichi. Wait till jeera turns golden.

3. Add onions. Stir fry till they turn light brown.
4. Add the vegetables (peas, carrots and beans) and salt. Stir fry for 3-4 minutes on medium flame.
5. Add rice and haldi. Mix gently. Add 2 cups of water. Boil.
6. After the boil, cover and cook on very low heat for 12-15 minutes, until the water is absorbed and the rice is done.

VARIATION :

Mushroom Pullao - *slice 100 gm mushrooms and use instead of the vegetables. Stir fry the onions until brown.*

Jeera Pullao - *Omit all vegetables and stir fry only the onions until rich brown.*

Soaking Rice...

Never soak rice. Always wash and strain. Leave them in the strainer for 30 minutes. Soaking makes the rice extra soft and sometimes the grains break while stirring them in oil.

Matar waale Chaawal

Serves 3-4

1 cup shelled peas (matar)
1 cup Basmati rice -wash well and strain keep in the strainer for 30 minutes
3 tbsp oil
1 tsp jeera (cumin seeds)
2 moti illaichi (brown cardamom)
4 laung (cloves)
1 tej patta (bay leaf)
1 tsp ginger paste
1¼ tsp salt or to taste

1. Wash the rice and strain. Keep in the strainer (channi) for 30 minutes. Drain rice and keep ready.
2. Heat 3 tbsp oil in a heavy bottomed deep pan. Reduce flame.
3. Add jeera, moti illaichi, laung and tej patta.
4. When jeera turns golden add ginger paste. Fry for 1 minute.
5. Add washed rice and peas. Stir fry gently for 1-2 minutes.
6. Add 2 cups water to the rice. Add salt.
7. Boil. After one boil cover with a well fitting lid and lower heat.
8. Cook for about 8-10 minutes on low heat, till all the water is absorbed and the rice gets well cooked. Fluff with a fork and serve hot.

Bhature

Makes 8

2 cups maida (plain flour)
1 cup suji (semolina)
½ tsp salt
½ tsp sugar
½ tsp soda-bi-carb (mitha soda)
½ cup sour curd
oil for deep frying

1. Soak suji in ¾ cup warm water, which is just enough to cover it. Keep aside for 10 minutes.
2. Sift salt, soda and maida in a paraat or a shallow bowl.
3. Add sugar, soaked suji and curd to the maida. Mix very well. Add warm water little by little, mixing well till the dough collects in the centre. Knead well to make a firm dough. Do not make it too soft as on keeping it turns loose.

4. Knead again with greased hands till the dough is smooth. Pat some oil on the dough to prevent it from drying. Grease a polythene with oil from inside and put the dough in it. Tie a knot loosely. Keep it in a warm place for 3-4 hours or till serving time.
5. Make 8-10 balls. Roll each ball to an oblong shape. Pull from one side to get a pointed tip.
6. Deep fry one at a time, in medium hot oil till crisp. Drain on paper napkins. Serve with channas.

Boondi Raita

Serves 4-5

2½ cups curd (½ kg)
1 cup boondi or besan ki pakori
1 tsp roasted cumin powder (bhuna jeera powder)
½ tsp chilli powder
½ tsp powdered sugar
salt to taste-½ tsp approx.

1. Beat curd. Mix all ingredients. Keep in the fridge till serving time.
2. Serve sprinkled with some bhuna jeera and red chilli powder.

Kheere ka Raita

2½ cups curd (½ kg)
1 small kheera - remove bitterness by rubbing ends with salt and grate without
peeling the green skin
½ tsp powdered sugar
salt to taste
¼ cup milk
1 tsp roasted jeera (cumin seeds) powder
½ tsp red chilli powder
¼ tsp kala namak
salt to taste

1. Beat curd very well. Add all the other ingredients. Mix well. Keep in the fridge till serving time.

Sweet Dishes

Gajar ka Halwa

Serves 4

½ kg carrot - washed nicely and grated into long shreds
1 cup milk, ¼ cup sugar, 2-3 tbsp desi ghee
5-6 badam (almonds) - shredded, 10-12 kishmish (raisins)
seeds of 3-4 chhoti illaichi (green cardamom) - powdered
100 gms khoya - grated

1. Boil 1 cup milk in a clean kadhai.
2. Add grated carrots and cook uncovered, stirring occasionally, till milk dries.
3. Add badam and kishmish. Stir for 1 minute.
4. Add sugar. Cook till the mixture turns dry again.
5. Add ghee and stir fry for 10 minutes on low flame.
6. Add grated khoya. Mix well. Serve hot.

Phirni

Serves 6

3½ cups (700 gm) milk
1/3 cup sugar (slightly less than ½ cup) or to taste
4 almonds (badam) - shredded
5-6 green pista (pistachio) - shredded
¼ cup basmati rice or rice flour
seeds of 2-3 chhoti illaichi (green cardamom) - powdered
1 drop kewra essence or 1 tsp ruh kewra
a few rose petals, optional

1. Soak rice of good quality for about an hour and then grind very fine with 4 to 5 tablespoonfuls of cold water (rice flour may be used as a substitute). Dissolve the rice paste in some more milk and make it thin.
2. Mix the rice paste with the milk in a heavy bottomed kadhai. Cook on medium heat, stirring continuously, till the mixture is of creamy consistency.
3. Add sugar and cardamom powder and stir.
4. Simmer till it is fully dissolved and then boil for 1 minute.
5. Remove from fire and add ruh kewra or the essence and half of the shredded almonds and pistachios.
6. Pour the mixture into 6 small glass bowls.
7. Chill. Decorate each dish with a few shredded nuts and rose petals.

Kheer

Serves 4-5

6 cups milk, preferably full cream, ¼ cup uncooked rice - wash & soak for ½ hour
¼ cup sugar
seeds of 3-4 chhoti illaichi (green cardamoms) - crushed to a powder
a few almonds - sliced thinly

1. Boil milk in a heavy bottomed kadhai. Drain rice and add to the boiling milk. Cook on low medium heat for 30 minutes, stirring frequently and mashing the rice grains. Keep scraping the milk on the sides too. Remove from fire.

2. Add sugar and illaichi powder. Mix well till sugar dissolves. Transfer to a serving dish. Garnish with almonds. Serve hot or cold.

REHEATING KHEER : *I had a very bad experience once with kheer. I was in a hurry to serve the kheer, so I put it on fire while I was doing something else also in the kitchen. I could not attend to it fully. It got burnt! The smoky flavour put off every one. The kheer should be reheated on very low heat and stirred constantly. Unattended kheer can be a disaster!*

Koftas in Green Gravy : Recipe on page 62 ➢

Recommended Oil-Olive Oil

- Olive oil is the only oil which is extracted from a fresh fruit, without the use of solvent. It is therefore a completely natural product with an exceptional aroma and flavour.
- Olive oil is perfect for all sorts of culinary purposes as it brings out the flavour of food. Olive oil can be used in its raw form, such as dressing for salads, sauces, soups, steamed or grilled vegetables, meat or fish and also when it is heated for toasting, stewing and frying.
- Olive oil expands on heating therefore less amount of olive oil is required while cooking. Unlike other oils, olive oil may be used 3-4 times, provided it is filtered carefully after each use through gauze, muslin cloth or a suitable paper filter.
- When used at high temperatures, olive oil forms a crisp, golden crust making the fried food appetizing and without affecting its nutritional value. During the process the oil hardly penetrates the food, leaving it light and digestible.
- Olive oil is the most stable of all oils, because of their extremely high oleic acid content (with average values between 75-80% and high polyphenol concentration, with alpha-tocopherol) which gives high natural protection against rancidity, guaranteeing stability under changing thermal conditions and preventing oxidation.
- Olive oil should be kept in a closed container, at room temperature and out of direct sunlight.

Health Benefts of Olive Oil

- Olive oil is highly recommended for its natural health benefits. The balanced fatty acid content helps you to maintain weight and is a recommended oil during diets.
- Other components such as natural antioxidants and vitamins A, D, K and especially E are also beneficial. As –
  1. They improve the appearance and smoothness of skin and hair.
  2. It lessens the severity of asthma and arthritis.
  3. It also has anti-inflammatory properties.
- One of the main benefits attributed to Olive Oil is that it reduces "bad" cholesterol (LDL) and retain "good" cholesterol (HDL). This helps prevent atherosclerosis and certain types of cancer.
- Because of its high oleic acid content, olive oil is well tolerated by the stomach and facilitates digestion.
- Olive oil is highly recommended for both the elderly and children.
  1. It is essential fatty acid content is similar to that of mother's milk and is assists in bone mineralization, development and calcification.
  2. Its high content of natural antioxidants creates a defence mechanism against oxidation process and improves cardiovascular circulation and slows down the ageing of cells.